FROM THE EDITORS:

Happy Holidays from all of us at Duncan Avenue! It's been an amazing year full of surprises and adventures. We are looking forward to 2018 and wishing you Happy Holidays!

- Max Loskutnikov & Dino Alexander

2017 / 2018

HOLIDAY GIFT GUIDE

COMING UP IN JANUARY: **WINTER TALES**

SELECT UNIQUE
DECOR GIFTS
FOR EVERYONE ON YOUR LIST

It's a common holiday conundrum: You want to show all your friends and family that you care, but finding the right present seems impossible. If you feel stuck, look for gifts that will enhance the home, because there is truly something for every personality. Skip the candle and coaster set and instead check out these unique, personal items that add fun and flair to any home, big or small.

❄ ❄ ❄ ❄ ❄

AQUARIUMS:

Traditional rectangular aquariums are bulky and cumbersome, but now there are stunning new tabletop options perfect for everyone on your list. The biOrb TUBE 15 aquarium is designed to give a 360-degree view and features multi-color LED lighting with remote control for an eye-catching way to enjoy fishkeeping. The TUBE 15 is also a low-maintenance gift given its 5-step filtration that maintains a clean, healthy aquatic environment to achieve ideal pH balance. Enjoy the dazzling sight of bubbling water and an impressive light show all year long.

❄ ❄ ❄ ❄ ❄

DECORATIVE PILLOWS + THROWS:

Winter is the perfect time to cozy up at home, but that tattered old blanket just won't do. You can encourage friends and family to get some much-needed R&R by gifting them new pillows and a fluffy throw blanket. Fun pillows are available in unique designs that feature different pictures, words or phrases, so it's easy to find something just right for that someone special. Add a coordinating throw blanket and get ready to cuddle through all of winter's chilliest nights.

❄ ❄ ❄ ❄ ❄

RESTORED PHOTOGRAPHS:

Going for tears of joy? One home decor gift that will tug at the heartstrings is framed photography. A nice portrait is always a great gift option, but this year surprise your loved ones by finding old photography and getting it restored. That photo of Grandpa fishing or of all your aunts as children is sure to bring back memories. Place in a nice frame and it is guaranteed to be an unforgettable gift that will be proudly displayed for years to come.

PERSONALIZED SIGNS:

One of the year's most popular decorating trends is custom signage. Often made from wood, these signs are painted or carved with your preferred message. That means it can be customized to suit even the most difficult people to shop for. Popular verbiage on a custom sign includes the family surname with an "established" date. You could also include a literary phrase or personal mantra that your loved one enjoys. Because the message is personalized, you can make it perfect for everyone on your list.

❄ ❄ ❄ ❄ ❄

HIMALAYAN SALT LAMPS:

When the holiday festivities are over, it's time to settle in and deal with Old Man Winter until springtime arrives. The soft glow of salt lamps brings a warmth to rooms on the dreariest days. Made from large pieces of salt, these lamps have an almost rock-like quality with veins of white, pink and peach throughout. Some people claim they also help maintain good indoor air quality and help with Seasonal Affective Disorder (SAD). No matter what, they are a happy addition to any room: bedroom, office or living room.

❄ ❄ ❄ ❄ ❄

THE PERSON WHO HAS EVERYTHING? CHECK. THE HARD-TO-SHOP-FOR TEEN? CHECK. THE NEWLYWED COUPLE SETTLING INTO THEIR HOME? CHECK. HOME DECOR GIFTS ARE GREAT FOR EVERYONE ON YOUR HOLIDAY GIFT LIST, AND BEST YET, THEY WON'T BE LIKE ANYTHING ELSE YOUR LOVED ONES RECEIVE, MAKING YOUR GIFT MEMORABLE & TRULY CHERISHED.

HUDSON VALLEY STYLE
DESIGNER PROFILE

Interview by Max Loskutnikov
ELISA FINOLI

Elisa: I'm a jewelry designer based in Red Hook, NY and the way I want my life and my business to impact the world around me is surely by being a responsible, attentive and resourceful person. It is not always easy and it comes with challenges and compromises, but it's our commitment to trying that

makes the difference. We are the decisions we make, the products we buy, the food we eat, the causes we believe in and fight for. All of this is a process, a learning process. In my business, too, it's a matter of choices and constant improvement. I make my creations using recycled gold and silver (or fairmined gold). Pearls and stones are also recycled/vintage or ethically sourced. I try to limit the use of chemicals as much as possible by using non-toxic alternatives. The packaging as well is sustainable and made of kraft boxes from recycled cardboard and 100% recyclable. No glue, no bleach and no dyes are used and the pouches are made from organic cotton. Giving back is another important aspect of my perception of the world and, even though my dream is to one day make a bigger impact, I started by supporting a project of victims of sex trafficking with small donations from the online purchases. I am aware it is a small gesture but, at least, it is one. Who knows how I will be able to help in the future!

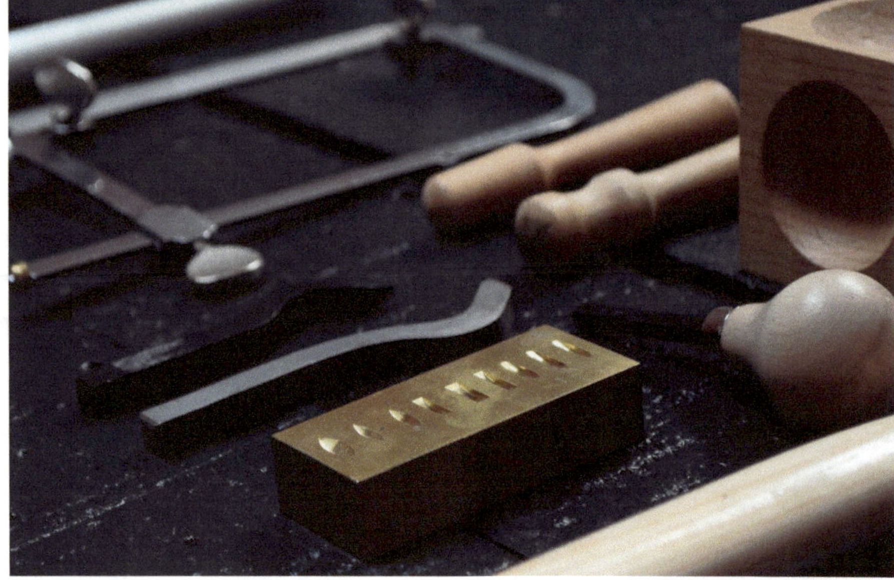

Elisa: Jewelry sort of simply happened. It showed itself as the synthesis of what expressed myself in the moment. I was probably ready to jump onto this new amazing adventure. I previously have learned a lot from various experiences I was lucky enough to have. Like in the architecture world where I was working on great design projects first in Milan, Italy, where it all started, then in London, UK with the well-known minimalist Claudio Silvestrin and finally in New York City. My passion for space, balance, clean

aesthetics, elegance, shapes, was temporarily put aside. I needed to give room to social, non-profit, cooperation, simplicity and supporting people, which brought me to live in India and Nicaragua getting involved in social work. The jewelry idea happened later, when I was looking for a sustainable piece with contemporary design for myself. It was hard and I was never satisfied with the offer, so I decided to give it a try. I studied what I needed to learn and started playing with it. I simply loved making jewelry and people loved my pieces. Suddenly it was a design process I was accustomed to matching with ecological and social values I believe in on a small and very creative scale. I find the inspiration for my pieces in the beauty of nature and organic forms but also in my architectural past. I experiment with textures, balance, opposites and I also get inspiration from the Japanese culture and the Wabi-Sabi philosophy. It's a philosophy based on finding beauty

in the imperfect. Imperfection becomes a form of freedom and acceptance, a celebration of nature.

Elisa: For years, I have been dedicating myself to design and architecture. So it was while working for the New York City firm Lang Architecture that I had the chance to get to better know the Hudson Valley. I was the interior designer for a beautiful housing development project in Kerhonkson called "Hudson Woods." I slowly discovered a new world made of amazing craftspeople, authenticity, incredible nature and wildlife, little villages where time and space were still an option. A few months, later my daughter was born and, with her, the desire for a different life. She was one and a half when we made our move upstate. At first it was both a bit scary and liberating but we are very happy now after two years living here.

Elisa: My perception is that the Hudson Valley Style is the perfect mix of genuineness and simplicity with some of New York City's more sophisticated and refined aspects. The Hudson Valley Style synthesizes what, in my opinion, is a good balanced style. There is history, there is nature, there is knowledge, there is art, there is respect, there is abstraction, there is culture, there is spirituality, there is elegance… all in one. This style is somehow very personal and eclectic. It's kind of difficult to describe it but, once you experience it, everything is clear.

Elisa: I honestly don't know what Aglaia Jewelry will become but I can tell you what I would love it to be. For sure, I want to work in a direction where the social help would go further than a donation and I would love for it to become a collaboration. But I need to grow and have more solid base. Aglaia Jewelry will surely try to be more and more conscious and to make clients proud of their choice. I also want to continue to grow in terms of my artistry. I feel the challenge but it's a very exciting one!

"I FIND THE INSPIRATION FOR MY PIECES IN THE BEAUTY OF NATURE AND ORGANIC FORMS BUT ALSO IN MY ARCHITECTURAL PAST"
ELISA FINOLI

TIPS FOR SETTING THE PERFECT HOLIDAY TABLE

Every holiday season, you invest hours planning and preparing the perfect menu for each celebration you host. While easy and fun may be the name of the game for buffet-style events, when it's a sit-down soiree, the delightful cuisine you produce deserves a presentation worthy of your efforts. A beautifully set table can elevate your holiday dinner from just great to simply perfect.

"Table-setting is an art form anyone can learn to execute beautifully," says Mary Bernardo, director of product development at Princess House, a leading provider of unique and exclusive cookware, food storage and home and entertainment products. "Simple touches like elegant holiday plates, colorful linens and an eye-catching centerpiece ensure a holiday table looks as inviting as the food smells."

Bernardo and the table decor experts at Princess House offer these tips for creating a beautiful holiday dinner table:

LAYERS LOOK LOVELY

Tablecloths, placemats, table runners and chargers not only help protect your table from spills and scrapes, but they also create a lovely backdrop for dishes, glasses, stemware and - of course - the food. Layering these items adds depth and interest to the tabletop.

Consider starting off with a simple white or red tablecloth, and then add either placemats in seasonal patterns or a festive runner. If chargers take up too much room on the table (or too much of your holiday budget), you can layer dinner and lunch plates to create the same effect. For example, place a Pavillion Berry Dinner Plate from Princess House beneath a Poinsettia Lunch Plate. The solid deep red of the dinner plate is the perfect complement to the elegant creamy background and poinsettia pattern of the lunch plate.

KEEP DISHWARE SEASONAL AND SIMPLE

"It's been said simplicity is the soul of elegance, and that's certainly true when you're setting a holiday dinner table," Bernardo says.

Choose dishes with a basic white or cream background accented with a traditional holiday motif. Flatware should also be simple; if your everyday collection is in good condition, feel free to use it for your holiday celebrations. If you don't have enough pieces, supplement with basic flatware that's free of embellishment or heavy designs. Glassware should also be simple and, whenever possible, multi-functional. For example, stemless wine glasses can be used for soft drinks and water, as well as wine.

ADD SEASONAL ACCENTS

Even the simplest table setting can feel festive when you add holiday-specific touches, like napkin rings in jewel green or red, a centerpiece filled with evergreen or holly and twinkling candles.

For a centerpiece that's festive and practical, consider using your favorite holiday serving bowl, such as a crystal bowl, for the foundation. Then add holiday decor items, like mini Christmas packages, your favorite Christmas tree decorations or a pillar candle in a holiday hue like red, green or snow white. Top with a few sprigs of evergreen, holly or fresh flowers and you have an easy, elegant DIY centerpiece.

Finally, don't overlook the opportunity to extend the table's festive atmosphere to the chairs as well. You can add to their elegance by adding simple decoration such as a mini-holiday wreath strung on a piece of ribbon and looped over the back of the chair.

"The dinner table is where holiday magic occurs," Bernardo says. "With a few special touches, you can set a holiday table that's perfect for the festive and welcoming spirit of the season."

Want to find more holiday decor and inspiration for the table? Visit www.princesshouse.com.

COASTING WHILE HOSTING:
5 WAYS TO KEEP YOUR HOLIDAY SPIRIT AT YOUR NEXT PARTY (BPT)

Many of us are already looking forward to hosting holiday gatherings this year - decorating our homes, whipping up festive foods, planning fun activities and surrounding ourselves with the warmth of family and friends.

In fact, one recent survey found 67 percent of U.S. consumers host and prepare food for holiday events, while another predicts we'll be spending an average $172 on such entertaining this season. As enjoyable as hosting is, however, the preparations can be time consuming. In a survey by Wakefield Research for BJ's Wholesale Club this year, 26 percent of U.S. respondents reported needing at least 24 hours to prepare for a holiday party. And trying to pull everything together can add pressure when we have copious other demands on our time.

"Our routines are interrupted by travel, guests, parties and the holidays themselves," notes physician Dr. Spencer Blackman in Entrepreneur. "If you're entertaining friends and family or organizing a work party, it takes upstream work to ensure a smooth event. Engage your support system and make a plan before things get crazy."

Consider these host-with-the-most suggestions for keeping the joy of the season no matter how large your impending event - and for making sure it's more fun than frantic.

SANTA KNOWS WHO'S ON THE NICE LIST.

You may be head elf, but there's no reason to take on every bit of the cooking, cleaning and entertaining yourself. Recruit a secondary elf squad ahead of time, assigning specific tasks so the work is parceled out evenly. Note: Youngsters needing gift-buying money may be motivated to take on the more grueling chores.

VISIONS OF SUGARPLUMS.

Plan your menu ahead. When you know way ahead of time what you'll be serving, most food items and utensils can be purchased in advance - and in volume - so you'll have plenty to offer even if your guest list spikes unexpectedly. The last thing you want is to run out; of the 65 percent of Americans who told Wakefield they've been at parties that went awry, 28 percent pointed to a shortage of eating utensils and 27 percent were disappointed

food ran out early. BJ's Wholesale Club has everything you need to stock up for your party - at incredible value.

REINDEER GAMES?

Check. Do the parents (and everyone else) at your gathering a favor by anticipating how your youngest party attendees will spend their time. Can you put together a kid-friendly craft, Lego, board game or cookie decorating table? Build a blanket fort? Set up age-appropriate video games? Rent movies? Stage a snowman-building contest? Put up port-a-cribs and baby swings for the nappers?

HAUL OUT THE HOLLY.

Fifty-six percent of Americans see decor as more impactful on holiday spirit than food, according to Wakefield. You can always go all out on decorations if that's your thing, but the most striking ones are often the simplest. Hang multiple strands of sparkling lights, add a fire to the fireplace, light sweet-smelling candles and generously place fresh red-ribboned pine boughs on mantles, around doorways and banisters and in containers. Nearly instant magic.

MIX AND A-MINGLE.

All too often, we're so busy making everything perfect for our guests we don't have time to join in the fun ourselves. The more you plan ahead to have your food, drinks and entertainment all planned out before guests arrive, the greater your chances of being able to relax and enjoy your own festivities.

The key to being a great host is to prepare enough so you're not hopelessly frazzled by the time guests arrive. Plan ahead this year so you can appreciate the joy of entertaining and create stellar holiday memories for all who attend. It may be the perfect ending of a perfect day.

Let BJ's Wholesale Club partner with you in providing all the fresh and frozen grocery items you need for your holiday soiree, in addition to decor, kitchen supplies and a cornucopia of gift ideas.

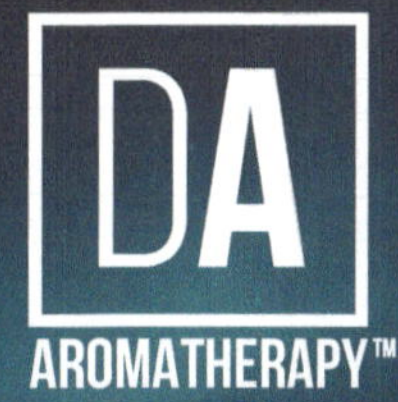

DA
AROMATHERAPY™

ENCOURAGING
AROMATHERAPY
[MIST]
····· with ·····
BLACK SPRUCE
& SANDALWOOD
ESSENTIAL OILS

BLACK ROCK FOREST™

DA-AROMATHERAPY.COM

THROW A HOLIDAY PARTY LIKE A PRO

As much as holidays are about tradition, many have an insatiable drive to outdo the festivities of years past and make this holiday season the most memorable yet.

How can you outshine yourself this holiday season? The answer is simple: Think big. Don't be confined to the party supplies you have around your house; stretch out and rent equipment like professional party planners use.

HERE ARE SOME IDEAS TO JUMP-START YOUR HOLIDAY PARTY PLANNING

SERVE YOUR FOOD THE RIGHT WAY

Preparing a holiday meal is a labor of love, but even for small gatherings, it can be a real challenge to make sure that delicious food stays warm and is served at its optimal temperature. Renting chafing dishes for main courses and hors d'oeuvres can ensure that the temperature and flavor of your food stays just right and that those masterpieces you cook up taste better than ever.

ADD SOME SMOKE, SNOW OR BUBBLES

Whether you want to bring some snow to a Christmas party or some cool smoke and fog effects to ring in the new year, renting a snow or smoke machine can create a party atmosphere like none other.

DRINK
IN STYLE

To throw a truly stellar holiday party, there are some items you must have. On the top of many people's list is a full-service bar. If you don't have a built-in bar in your home or party venue, you're in luck. Why? Because you'll have more options to choose from when you decide to rent one. Whether it's an illuminated bar, modernist style or a classic stone-top design, renting a portable bar to fit your party is key.

FOUNTAINS
OF DELICIOUSNESS

To really go all out, you need to think bigger. You need to plan as though you were throwing an A-list celebrity party. Renting a champagne or chocolate fountain is a sure way to do this. A perfect blend of luxury and deliciousness, a fountain will leave guests talking about that tumbling tower of liquid chocolate or bubbling champagne for years to come.

FOCUS ON
THE DETAILS

For many holiday get-togethers, it's all about having the right plates and serving ware. For a reasonable price, you can easily rent fine china and exquisite glassware that will wow your guests. Best of all, you won't have to spend a fortune on items you only use a couple of times a year!

Visit www.RentalHQ.com
for more holiday party ideas.

UNDERCURRENT BRACELET
$198
SARAGOLDEN.COM

LAPEL PIN TRIO
$40
SARAGOLDEN.COM

STAR SIGNET RING, AQUAMARINE
$128
SARAGOLDEN.COM

A trio of brass pins: a Sparkling Stone Pin featuring a hand holding a genuine moonstone, the Golden Pin, and the Gem Pin. Put them together for instant flair, or keep one and gift the rest to your besties.

Classic and architectural, this bracelet features rows of sleek snake chain stacked next to one another to form a flowy, composed look. Available in extra thick 14k gold or silvery rhodium plating.

A classic signet ring featuring a single star and genuine aquamarine stone. In solid brass or sterling silver with an antiqued finish, the blackened star makes the aquamarine shine extra bright.

Sara Golden

SARAGOLDEN.COM

5 EASY WAYS TO TURN YOUR HOUSE INTO A SMART HOME

(BPT) - There was a time when setting up a smart home was a labor-intensive endeavor. You had to know which devices worked together, spend tedious days getting everything to work just right, then master complicated software to control the whole experience.

Things have changed. Nowadays, smart homes are more sophisticated than ever. You can set up your entire home right from your smartphone, and everything can be controlled by your voice.

That's right, you don't need to know any codes or remember any complex steps to reap the benefits of a smart home. Do you want to dim the lights for movie night, listen to your favorite album while cooking dinner or turn on the lawn sprinklers without leaving the couch? All you have to do is ask.

At the center of a smart home is a voice service like Amazon Alexa on the Echo, Echo Dot or Echo Show, which allows you to control more than 1,000 devices using just your voice. You can connect to as many or as few smart devices as you want. Services like Alexa also let you access the latest news and weather, set reminders and even order dinner for the night.

For a sample of what's possible with a smart home, here are five devices that can lead you to a whole new home experience!

WEMO MINI SMART PLUG.

This Wi-Fi-enabled plug can transform almost every appliance in your home into a voice-enabled device. Plug your coffee maker, lamp or fan into it, then simply pair it with your voice service. With just a simple command like "Alexa, start the coffee," you'll soon smell the heavenly aromas of fresh-brewed java.

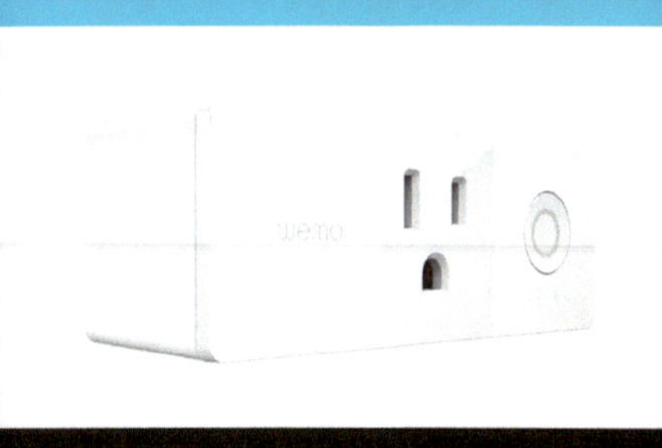

TP-LINK MULTICOLOR LED BULB.

There are light bulbs, and then there are smart bulbs. This LED bulb contains multiple colors, from warm reds to cool blues, plus hundreds of other shades and tints that allow you to light your space according to the mood or occasion, all through a simple voice command.

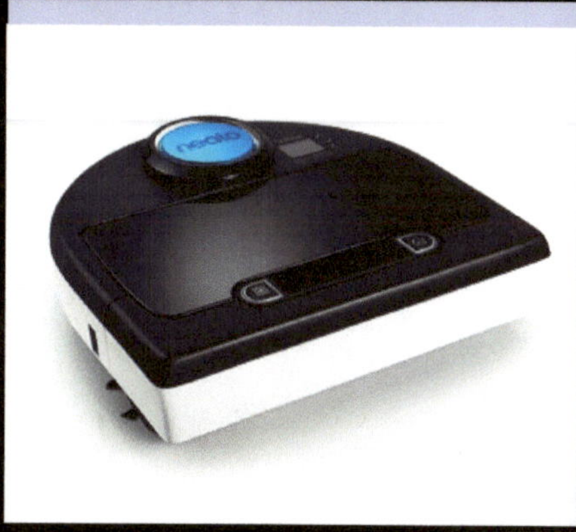

NEATO BOTVAC.

Not too many people like cleaning, so when they hear there's a Wi-Fi-enabled robot vacuum that automatically cleans floors for you, their ears perk up. Connect the Neato Botvac to your Amazon Alexa and voila, cleaning the floors is as easy as, "Alexa, ask Neato to start cleaning."

ECOBEE4 SMART THERMOSTAT.

Smart thermostats are wildly popular for the simple reason that they save homeowners money. If you forget to turn down the heat when you step out, you can do so from your smartphone. With sensors that manage hot and cold spots, easy programming features and more, this smart thermostat can save you an average of 23 percent on heating and cooling costs each year.

AMAZON ECHO, ECHO DOT OR ECHO SHOW.

A smart home is not just about smart devices, it's also about making your life easier. For instance, if you're throwing a dinner party and want music to set the mood, just ask "Alexa, play jazz music." The same is true if you want to check the weather, order food for a night in or see what's on your calendar for the day. If you find you're out of laundry detergent or cooking oil, you can easily order by asking Alexa to have it delivered to your home. All you have to do is ask.

The beauty of a smart home is that you can pick and choose the features you want. Whether you want to clean, adjust the lighting or listen to your favorite song, with a voice service like Amazon Alexa and Amazon Echo, you'll experience convenience and the fruits of technology in a whole new way.

The holidays are a wonderful time of year to spend with family and friends, and to reconnect with those you may not often see. However, the festive season can also be a busy and expensive time. By January, many are left feeling exhausted physically, emotionally and financially. But don't

5 HACKS TO SAVE TIME AND MONEY DURING THE HOLIDAYS

let the stress of the season stand in the way of the magic - follow these easy tips and tricks to enjoy a more relaxing and joyful holiday season.

❄ MAKE A LIST:

And check it twice! Getting organized this holiday season can save you time and money. When shopping for holiday gifts, having a complete list before you enter the store can prevent you from browsing the aisles for items you do not need. You will also have an estimated total cost before shopping, so you can stick to your budget.

❄ SEND E-CARDS:

It is always exciting to receive holiday mail from loved ones, but between the postage and printing fees, sending your own cards can quickly add up. Sending e-cards, however, is a more cost-effective approach and you can send as many as you'd like! You can also apply the money you save to your gifting budget.

❄ SWITCH TO STRAIGHT TALK:

From searching seasonal recipes to online shopping, there is no better helper than a smartphone during the holiday season. Straight Talk Wireless recently launched its new Ultimate Unlimited Plan for just $55 per month - helping you tackle the holidays and stream your favorite videos at DVD quality, without worrying about running out of high speed data. Never get throttled again. So treat yourself to the gift of unlimited data by switching to Straight Talk Wireless, the leading no-contract wireless provider that offers customers the best phones on the best networks for less. With no contracts, no credit checks and no mystery fees, your phone bill will be one less cost to worry about this season.

❄ WRAP LIKE A PRO:

Gift wrapping can be one of the most time consuming activities of the holidays. However, there are multiple hacks to expedite the wrapping process. For oddly shaped gifts - use Kraft paper bags and decorate with a silver paint marker. You can also spruce up plain wrapping paper using twine, ribbons and stencils. Be creative if you run out of supplies, in the end it is the thought that matters, not the presentation!

❄ MONITOR FOR DEALS:

Online holiday shopping has made it easy to avoid the craze of the mall. But another added benefit of shopping from home is finding ways to avoid paying full price. Once you reach the checkout page, do a quick online search for discount codes for that particular site. You will be shocked to find how simple it is to save a few extra bucks or even snag free shipping!

MAKE IT A PRIORITY THIS YEAR TO NOT LOSE THE SPIRIT OF THE SEASON WITHIN THE HUSTLE AND BUSTLE. WHILE THEY MAY SEEM SIMPLE, THESE FEW STEPS WILL HELP YOU PUT AN END TO THE POST-HOLIDAY SLUMP BEFORE IT HITS.

(BPT)

THE APOTHECARY DELUXE
by Hudson Made New York

The Complete works from face to feet. Hudson Made exclusive Apothecary Box with all new Rose Liquid Hand Soap and a beautiful ceramic dish by Dana Brandwein at DBO Home. Finally, luxurious pampering encapsulated in one chic package!

HUDSONMADENY.COM

$148.00

BOTANICAL BAR TRIO
by The Hudson Standard

Three of the favorite Hudson Valley Style bitters in 1 oz. size bottles are samples of the fantastic ways bitters add depth and flavor to drinks and cooking. Ginger, Spruce Shoot and Catskill Masala will have you covered for numerous cocktail recipes that call for spice, citrus or aromatic bitters. The sturdy modern packaging makes a great gift and easy to ship.

THEHUDSONSTANDARD.COM

$24.00

NATURAL TRAVEL SET
by DA Aromatherapy Collection

DA-AROMATHERAPY.COM

$34.00

Experience the Magic of Hudson Valley anywhere you go! Your body deserves only the best skin care products and DA Aromatherapy Collection crafted them in the convenient travel size. Makes a perfect Hudson Valley Style gift too!

Hudson Valley
THERE IS NO PLACE LIKE HOME, AND OUR HOME IS THE MOST BEAUTIFUL PLACE ON EARTH. BROWSE OUR STORE FOR HUDSON VALLEY INSPIRED DESIGN.
LEARN MORE
Reclaimed Wood 52" Side Table
$1,400.00
BUY NOW
DUNCANAVENUE.COM

Vacation is supposed to be fun and relaxing, but more than half of Americans say vacations cause them stress, and 46 percent say stress interferes with their enjoyment of traveling, according to a survey by HomeAway. Vacation stress comes from crowded airports, making transportation arrangements, booking lodging and more.

However, staying organized while traveling can help relieve some of the stress of juggling so many details. These tips will help you stay organized while traveling, and feel more confident and in control of your vacation plans.

PRIOR TO DEPARTURE

MAKE AN ITINERARY
with important information, such as flight numbers and times, hotel phone numbers, check-in and check-out times, prices, ticket numbers and phone numbers for attractions you'll visit.

GATHER
together travel guide info. If you're still a fan of paper, create a packet of travel guides and maps for the area you'll be visiting. Or go electronic and download guides and maps on your smartphone.

REMEMBER
to make arrangements for your home while you're away. Discontinue newspaper and mail delivery, put lights on timers and ask the local police department to do vacation checks on your home.

PACKING ORGANIZATION

PACK
a few days before your departure. Waiting until the last minute to pack can make you feel rushed and stressed - and increase the chance you'll forget something important.

MAKE A CHECKLIST
of everything you need to take with you and check off each item as it goes into your bags. Organize your checklist by when items can be packed - well in advance (for seasonal clothes you don't need at home) to last-minute (toiletries).

PLAN OUTFITS
and take items that can be mixed and matched with each other.

Before critical items go into your bags, outfit them with technology that will help you keep track of them, like the TrackR pixel, a coin-sized item tracker that attaches to items from car and house keys to wallets, passport cases to handbags. The TrackR smartphone app works with the item tracker to help locate the tagged items.

ON THE ROAD

If you're traveling with the whole family and have a lot to carry, consider making each person responsible for a different, age-appropriate, item. For example, parents can manage large bags, teens and tweens can handle carry-on items and young children can be responsible for any small entertainment or comfort items, such as stuffed animals and carry-ons with coloring books and Crayons.

KEEP

all passports in one place and have a single, responsible party manage them.

CARRY

a small journal to help keep track of notes about places you go, changes in plans or reservations, receipts, tickets and more.

PACK

a small bag for snacks and water. Vacation travel often involves waiting, whether at the airport for a delayed flight or in line for a popular attraction. A small snack bag can help prevent hunger-fueled frustration and lack of focus.

SOME STRESS WHILE TRAVELING MAY BE UNAVOIDABLE, BUT STAYING ORGANIZED WHILE ON VACATION CAN HELP ENSURE YOU FEEL AS LITTLE STRESS AS POSSIBLE - AND LEAVE YOU PLENTY OF ENERGY TO ENJOY YOUR TRIP.

MEOW MEOW TWEET // MIGRATOR KIT
$48 // MEOWMEOWTWEET.COM

A collection of travel friendly toiletries for you and your flock.

Whether you're flying South, looking for the perfect gift or want to try our best sellers, this kit is for you! Enjoy a complete facial and body care regime to cleanse, moisturize and nourish your skin.

CAPTAIN BLANKENSHIP
MERMAID HAIR CARE SET
$75 // CAPTAINBLANKENSHIP.COM

Our popular Mermaid Hair Care Products (Full Size Sea Salt Hair Spray, Dry Shampoo & Hair Oil) nestled in the cutest box imaginable. This trio will add texture, life and moisture to your hair while keeping it looking fresh between washes. This is all you need for beachy mermaid hair! Makes a great gift for yourself or loved ones.

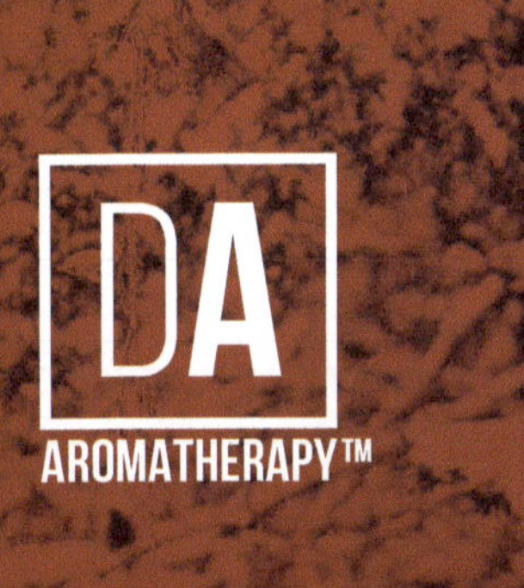

ENERGIZING
AROMATHERAPY
MIST
with
ORANGE
& PEPPERMINT
ESSENTIAL OILS

SUMMER BLISS™

DA-AROMATHERAPY.COM

DA
AROMATHERAPY™

SOOTHING AROMATHERAPY MIST WITH ORGANIC EUCALYPTUS & PEPPERMINT ESSENTIAL OILS - FEEL AWESOME™

by DA Aromatherapy Collection

Experience the soothing power of Organic Eucalyptus & Peppermint Essential Oils. DA Aromatherapy Hudson Valley-inspired Centering Body Mist and Aromatherapy Spray with Organic Eucalyptus Globulus Essential Oil and Organic Peppermint Essential Oils is part of DA Aromatherapy's natural, paraben-free, sulfate-free, vegan skin care product line made with plant derived ingredients, designed and crafted in Hudson Valley, New York.

DA-AROMATHERAPY.COM

$7.00-9.00

CREATE YOUR OWN CUSTOM AROMATHERAPY MIST

by DA Aromatherapy Collection

Create Your Own Natural Fragrance / Aromatherapy Mist with Organic Essential Oils! DA Aromatherapy Collection gives you the power to be your own natural fragrance & aromatherapy designer at your fingertips.

1. Select Your Top Notes

These are the first and most noticeable notes when you first smell the fragrance and include fresh, clean and sparkling citrus and herbaceous, grassy and minty essential oils.

2. Select Your Mid (or Heart) Notes

They open up your natural fragrance's true character, last longer, make a bigger impression and include floral, fruity and spicy essential oils.)

3. Select Your Base (or Dry Down) Notes

They are Earthy, Woodsy, Musky and ground your natural fragrance, balance it and make it last longer.

DA Aromatherapy Collection Essential Oil Mists is the easiest way to enjoy all the benefits of Aromatherapy on the go. Simply use it as your body mist or a refreshing room spray and lift up your mood any time and anywhere!

DA-AROMATHERAPY.COM

$17.00

NATURAL HAND SANITIZERS WITH ORGANIC ESSENTIAL OILS

by DA Aromatherapy Collection

Protect yourself and loved ones plus get aromatherapy boost on the go with these natural hand sanitizers. DA Aromatherapy's Hand Sanitizing Mists with Organic Essential Oils are effective against 99.9% of common germs and bacteria.

DA-AROMATHERAPY.COM

$7.00

Sara Golden

SARAGOLDEN.COM

DA
AROMATHERAPY™

CENTERING
[AROMATHERAPY
MIST]
with
LAVENDER
& CEDARWOOD
ESSENTIAL OILS
MOUNTAIN BREEZE™
DA-AROMATHERAPY.COM

STRESS-BUSTING
SPEED-CLEANING TIPS
FOR THE HOLIDAYS
(BPT)

It's no secret the holiday season can be one of the busiest and most stressful times of the year. What is one of the biggest sources of stress? It's cleaning on a deadline, especially while guests are on their way.

But with the right plan in place, even last-minute pre-entertainment cleaning can be efficient and stress-free, says Debra Johnson, Merry Maids home cleaning expert.

In an online survey conducted this spring by Toluna, more than half of respondents admitted that most of their cleaning takes place just before guests arrive. With a bit more focus, this preparation can be quick and effective, without stress. After all, the holidays shouldn't be a race against the clock. They're about spending time with loved ones.

Johnson shares the following tips to clean smarter, not harder, in the limited time you have before guests arrive.

1. READY, SET ... DECLUTTER

The important first step is to declutter rooms. Set a timer if needed to help you stay on track and avoid spending too much time in one room. Put things where they belong, or if they don't have a home, put them in a room or under beds where no one will see. Once the holiday season passes, you can revisit and declutter those hidden storage areas. Prioritize rooms you use most, so if you run out of time, guests won't notice an untidy area.

2. ONLY CLEAN WHAT GUESTS WILL SEE

Join the more than one-third of Americans who don't bother cleaning rooms people won't see. You have enough to stress about as the host. Don't waste your precious time cleaning parts of the home no one will ever see. Simply shut doors to rooms that you want to keep private, signaling to guests not to enter. If you have family staying with you, give guest rooms a once-over, clean the bathrooms that will be used and, of course, the kitchen and living room.

3. SKIP THE SWEEP

Don't spend time sweeping with a dry mop when you can vacuum instead. Vacuuming is far more efficient and faster at removing dust, dirt and other debris from the floors. Keep a portable hand-held vacuum nearby in case a big mess happens, such as a glass breaking during a party. Within seconds, the mess will be gone and you can go back to enjoying the festivities.

4. SPEED-CLEAN THE BATHROOMS

All you need to clean your bathroom quickly is a damp microfiber cloth to give every surface a quick wipe-down and a toilet brush to clean the inside walls of the toilet. To freshen it up even more, pour a half-cup of baking soda into the toilet bowl and add white vinegar along with a few drops of your favorite essential oils. Allow the mixture to bubble for a bit and scrub with a toilet brush. Then, voila: your bathroom is clean, shiny and smelling great.

5. TACKLE THE MICROWAVE MESS

You know people will want seconds well after the leftovers are put away, so use this quick tip to tackle microwave build-up: Combine lemon juice and water in a microwave-safe bowl and run it for about two minutes. The lemon water will loosen any gunk or food in the microwave for an easy wipe down with a microfiber cloth. Now guests can reheat their leftovers in a clean microwave.

"Hosting a holiday dinner requires prep work, but if you stay on track before anyone arrives, you can spend more time actually relaxing and enjoying their company," said Johnson.

If you simply don't have any time to spare this holiday season, Merry Maids has the resources and experts to help. Find a location in your area by visiting www.merrymaids.com.

WITH THE CLEANING UNDER CONTROL, ALL THAT'S LEFT FOR YOU TO DO IS TO LIGHT A FEW CANDLES, CONQUER THE GROCERY LIST AND, OF COURSE, ENJOY YOUR SPECIAL GUESTS.

PUNTO&BACCHETTA
IN SOLID 14K GOLD AND STERLING SILVER
$715
AGLAIAJEWELRY.COM

Punto e Bacchetta Ring, with its coral-like details, has a simple design and strong style. It is essential, yet sophisticated.

BOTTONE EARRINGS
IN SOLID STERLING SILVER
$130
AGLAIAJEWELRY.COM

These simple yet unique studs are the size of a medium button. Minimal but full of character, they're perfect for any style.

Also available in 14K Gold

FLAT RING
IN SOLID 14K GOLD
$435
AGLAIAJEWELRY.COM

Flat Ring, featuring a flat top design, offers a modern and minimalist detail to any look. It's wonderful as a single piece but also suitable for stacking.

Also available in Sterling Silver

aglaïa

BARN DOORS GO INDOORS: AN IDEAL WINTER PROJECT

(BPT)

Known for their versatility, barn doors have been popping up in homes across the country - in contemporary and rustic designs. Read on to discover why adding a barn door is an ideal winter home-improvement project.

TRANSITIONS IN OPEN FLOOR PLANS

As homeowners seek more open floor plans, interior doors are evolving. Barn doors meet homeowners' desire for fluid room flows by seamlessly connecting adjacent rooms, allowing the flexibility to close spaces off or join them.

"The rolling feature of barn doors creates a fresh look in any home," says Brad Loveless, product development manager for Simpson Door Company. "The functionality of a door mounted on a barn track allows homeowners to control the degree to which spaces are opened or closed." Unlike conventional hinge-mounted doors, barn doors open previously divided rooms with an air of intentionality.

SHOWCASING STYLE AND PERSONALITY

Like a distinctive piece of art in the home, the right interior door can showcase a homeowner's style and personality. An unexpected door style creates a great discussion point when entertaining friends and family. Is your home lacking a statement piece that inspires creativity and sparks conversation? You may find that a barn door is a simple solution to this problem with its eye-catching rolling feature.

ADAPTABLE TO CHANGING STYLE TRENDS

Do you ever worry that the sweater you bought last week will be out of style in a year or two? Are you a trend skeptic since the bell-bottom era? (If those can go out of style, anything can, right?) These farmyard-meets-indoors statement pieces have actually been around for over a decade. Today you'll find barn doors with a modern, sleek look, rustic wood paneling or even made with a chalkboard.

Barn doors are available from several companies. For homeowners who like the look and feel of wood doors, Simpson Door Company offers rustic-style barn doors, as well as sleek, contemporary doors that can be mounted on barn track hardware.

WHY NOW?

Adding a barn door while you're stuck inside for the cold months makes an immediate visual difference in your home and can provide a scenic backdrop for holiday photos.

aglaïa

DA
AROMATHERAPY™

CALMING
AROMATHERAPY
[MIST]
with
LAVENDER
& CHAMOMILE
ESSENTIAL OILS
ZEN GARDEN™
DA-AROMATHERAPY.COM

THE GIFT OF HEALTH

DR. ERIK BROWER
& INNATE CHIROPRACTIC

Interview by Maxwell Alexander

Max: Hi, Erik! Thank you for the cover story in our first holiday issue! It was a life changing experience for both Dino and I to find out about Innate Chiropractic. Please tell our readers about yourself, what you do and the role your practice plays in the local community.

Dr. Erik: Innate Chiropractic was founded in Newburgh, New York in November of 2010. Our mission is to assist individuals and families in gaining victory over their health and having better lives through neurologically based chiropractic care; building healthier communities for generations to come. We believe in community outreach, treating people the way we would want to be treated, and helping our practice members attain the best lives possible. At Innate, we welcome all people from newborn infants to centurions, high level athletes, people who have tried everything and lost hope, and people looking to maintain, prevent, or enhance their health to its highest potential. We are proud to offer a refreshing, natural and different approach to health care.

Max: Why did you decide to make Hudson Valley your home and start your practice here?

Dr. Erik: Where to practice, spend our time and raise our family was such an important decision for my wife and myself. While in chiropractic school we would go on long road trips checking out areas in the country that we thought we may want to live. I was from a small town in the Catskills and my wife Dana from Long Island. South Florida and Northern California topped our list, with New York about last on our list at the time. We actually settled on a town outside of San Francisco and at the last minute had a "God moment" and knew immediately we wanted to go back to New York and be closer to family. Once settled upon New York we thought about what was most important to us as far as location and conveniences and decided the Hudson Valley and specifically Orange County is where we should be. We opened in 2010 and could not be happier. We love the people and find something new and amazing in the Hudson Valley almost weekly.

MY GOAL WAS TO MAKE AN INSPIRING SPACE FOR OUR TEAM AND COMMUNITY.

We hired a designer to help make our dream a reality. The designer was so instrumental in guiding us and helping me make tough decisions. The best part is that everyone really seems to love the office and its details. The biggest compliment I get is when people tell us that the office feels warm and inviting.

Design: Sweet Life Design
Custom desk and doors: The Orchard Group
GC: Tripple R development

Max: Sounds great! And what about
your personal style?

Dr. Erik: I can always remember style being
important to me. I would describe my personal
office attire as comfortable, muted, fitting with
some edge. I believe we show respect to others
by how we present ourselves, so I always want
to look professional, but still stay true to me. I
have to be able to move so pants and shirts that
have stretch to them are always a plus. I have
also become a creature of habit and don't like to
spend a lot of time with my clothing choices, so
I don't wear a lot of patterns or bright colors and
will buy a handful of the same items in different
colors to keep it simple.

Max: Everyone is looking forward to holidays
and the New Year. What is your advice to our
readers for this holiday season and how to make
New Year the best year of their lives.

Dr. Erik: A quote I love is, "Your body's ability
to adapt, heal and thrive is far greater than you
have been led to believe." At Innate we have
seen people heal naturally at such high rates
that I cannot believe how absolutely amazing
our bodies and healing potentials are. Evaluate
what is most important to you regarding your
health and then find the very best professionals
or plan, based on results, to help you reach
it. Once you find that person or plan, honor
yourself by being consistent and never giving
up on yourself.

" I BELIEVE WE SHOW RESPECT TO OTHERS BY HOW WE PRESENT OURSELVES, SO I ALWAYS WANT TO LOOK PROFESSIONAL, BUT STILL STAY TRUE TO ME"

DR. ERIK BROWER

Photographer: Yachin Parham
Stylist: Chelsea Volpe
Hair & Makeup: Alfred Lester
Model: Anniek Amba

aglaïa

TRIA EARRINGS // FROM $141.00
AGLAIAJEWELRY.COM

Triangle. In art, architecture, life. "The alchemical/magical symbol for water is an inverted triangle, symbolizing downward flow.

The downward pointing triangle is an ancient symbol of femininity.
One of the four alchemical elements, water has the properties cold and moist, and symbolizes intuition, the unconscious mind, and the enclosing, generating forces of the womb."

Tria earrings have simple lines and minimal look. They can complement any style with a glamorous twist.

Showing Tria earrings in 14K recycled Gold and recycled Sterling Silver.

Imperfections and variations are part of the handmade charm, and to be expected.

HUDSON VALLEY
STYLE
MAGAZINE
ADVERTISE.
HUDSON VALLEY STYLE.
INFO@HUDSONVALLEYSTYLEMAGAZINE.COM

DA AROMATHERAPY NATURAL
HAND SANITIZERS

DA AROMATHERAPY
COLLECTION BY DUNCANAVENUE

MADE IN
USA

NATURALLY DERIVED ESSENTIAL OILS

DESIGNED & CRAFTED IN HUDSON VALLEY
DA-AROMATHERAPY.COM

4 LAUNDRY PERSONALITIES:

WHERE DO YOU FIT?

(BPT) - Chic, trendy, sporty, bohemian, sophisticated, fun, classic - you probably have a clear vision of your fashion and style personality. But do you know your laundry personality? How you wash the clothes you wear is every bit as personal and unique to you as the clothes themselves. Knowing your laundry personality could help ease the load and make the chore easy and fail-proof.

A quarter of American households say they overload their washer most of the time, according to a survey commissioned by LG Electronics. Even people who say they are doing their laundry efficiently still have complaints with the process. In fact, more than three-fourths believe washers can be improved.

Recognizing your laundry personality and choosing products that cater to your unique style will make doing laundry an easy, and perhaps even enjoyable, affair! Here are four common laundry personalities, their identifying traits, and tips for achieving maximum efficiency:

THE LIGHT LOADER

Does your desire to separate and preserve clothes, including those delicate special care items, ever leave you with the only option of running the washer with just one or two items? You're not alone. According to a recent survey commissioned by LG Electronics, 60 percent of Americans admitted to running a full load of laundry for six items or less.

The LG TWINWash system will put an end to that, letting consumers tackle two loads of laundry at once, or independently. The industry-first two-in-one washing machine includes a front-load washer ergonomically placed on the top for larger loads, and a smaller washer, the LG Sidekick, which sits within the pedestal for those small specialty loads. The LG SideKick provides an additional 1-foot capacity and has six cycles to choose from: normal, intimates, hand wash, active wear, rinse + spin and tub clean, allowing consumers to wash those smaller loads, saving time and energy.

THE SUPER SORTER

Does the thought of washing dark jeans and a pink blouse in the same load leave you light-headed? You and 20 percent of Americans prefer to avoid mixing items of different colors in the same load. Some of those surveyed also don't trust washing items like delicates (52 percent), jackets (49 percent) and blouses (30 percent) in the main wash.

Facilitate your separation efforts by using multiple baskets or hampers in your laundry room. Label them - darks, whites, delicates, workout, etc. - and encourage family members to drop their dirty clothes in the appropriate basket. For items not trusted for the main wash, the LG SideKick, part of the TWINWash system, can help tackle smaller loads, ensuring they're properly washed by one of the six cycles.

THE DUMPER

Do you do minimal separation? You're joined by a majority of Americans that load up their washer. A recent survey concluded that 80 percent of Americans have purposely overloaded their washer to avoid doing a second load of laundry. Plus, 22 percent of Americans have deemed clothes not properly cleaned because of an overloaded washer. High-efficiency front-load washing machines alleviate both of these problems. Unlike traditional top-load washing machines with agitators, front-load washers offer greater capacity while using much less water, which actually cleans clothes better! It's a myth that more water equals cleaner clothes. Plus, they have faster spin speeds than their top-load counterparts, which means your clothes come out dryer, saving you time and energy when drying your clothes.

THE HABITUAL DRY CLEANER

Summer is a busy - and sticky - time, running from work to outdoor barbecues during the hottest months of the year. And refreshing that summer wardrobe between pool parties is key to the habitual dry cleaner looking and feeling their best. That's where the LG Styler comes in. The LG Styler is a fashion-forward, one-of-a-kind clothing management system that can refresh and sanitize clothing in as little as 20 minutes. Just get back from an outdoor cocktail party? Simply place your favorite dresses, shirts or suits inside and let LG's TrueSteam technology work its magic to reduce wrinkles and odors from things like sweat or smoke, without any harsh chemicals. While it doesn't replace dry cleaning, it can certainly help reduce trips to the cleaners while keeping your clothes crisp and ready to go before your next brunch date or happy hour.

Whatever your laundry personality, you can find a washer, dryer and detergent that will make your chore easier and less time consuming. Then, you can spend that time on other things. In fact, Americans surveyed say if they could cut their laundry time in half, they'd spend that extra time hanging out with their kids, watching TV or doing other things they enjoy.

HUDSON VALLEY
STYLE
MAGAZINE

POWER TO YOU
& Your Creativity
CREATE YOUR OWN
BLEND
CHOOSE FROM
30+ ORGANIC
ESSENTIAL OILS
da-aromatherapy.com

DA AROMATHERAPY
COLLECTION BY DUNCAN AVENUE

MADE IN
USA

NATURALLY DERIVED ESSENTIAL OILS

DESIGNED & CRAFTED IN HUDSON VALLEY